Drum Set Development
L2

Composed by Giovanni Andreani

First published in 2022 by
GA
Via Colombo 4, 24061 Albano Sant'Alessandro, BG, Italy
Copyright © Giovanni Andreani 2015
ISBN 978-88-314710-2-2
All rights reserved. No part of this publication may be reproduced, stored
in any retrieval system, or transmitted, in any form or by any means,
electronic, mechanical, photocopying, recording or otherwise, without the
prior written permission of the copyright owner.

To André Arpino

"Elemental Music is never just music. It's bound up with movement, dance and speech, and so it is a form of music in which one must participate, in which one is involved not as a listener bust as a co-performer."

— Carl Orff

PREFACE

A comprehensive and effective programme must consider all of the possible sectors in which the student's skills and competence can develop, which fall into two main categories: musicianship[1] and instrumental skills. The Music Method Project (MusMP) comprises the Percussion Method Project (PercMP), related to the development of instrumental skills, and the Musicianship Method Project (MMP), related to musicianship development.

While musicianship will develop slightly when studying an instrument, scientifically well-programmed musicianship development will be the primary factor for excellent instrumental improvement. As a consequence, some areas of development in PercMP will be performed at one drum or a set of drums, while others will have to be undertaken with or without the subsidiary use of a drum (see footnote 3).

The more the proposed activities[2] are varied and systematically organised, the better the development of skills and competence will be. As a consequence, the contrast between different activities will stimulate the student's interest, which will result in greater emotional involvement, a higher level of participation, and a more dynamic attitude.

Differentiation must also consider the time terms that are intrinsic to all specific Development Areas.

In PercMP, the following time terms have been conceived:

- Instant Term [IT] – from 5 seconds to 15 minutes
- Daily Term [DT] – 15 minutes to 6 hours
- Very Short Term [VST] – 1 day to 1 week
- Short Term [ST] – 2 weeks
- Medium Term [MT] – 1 month
- Long Term [LT] – 2 to 4 months
- Very Long Term [VLT] – 4 to 6 months

Within a well-differentiated programme, the student should deal simultaneously with activities that require different time terms that derive from different areas. Short-term activities should

---

1 *Musicianship should be considered essential for the student's improvement; in many cases it is not, for many reasons, among which lies the complexity to plan a specific, comprehensive curriculum.*
2 *Refer to 'List of Abbreviations' at the end of the introduction for this and other specific terms.*

outnumber those that are expected to take longer.

Although it is undoubtedly important for the student to simultaneously manage various activities as part of the different areas of development, any new activity should be gradually introduced.

Within PercMP, Snare Drum Development (SDD), along with Drum Set Development (DD) are the only Development Areas that should be constantly active: all other areas can be started according to the teacher's discretion, in relation to the student's aptitude, specific needs, expectations, and so forth.

In PercMP, the Development Areas are (with their corresponding time terms):

- Snare Drum Development [VST]
- Drumset Development [VST]
- Sing & Play[3] for percussionists [VST]
- Note Reading[3] [IT] – [VST]
- Listen & Play[3] for percussionists [IT] – [VST]
- Sight Reading [IT]
- Rudiment Exercises [ST] – [VLT]
- Études [MT] – [VLT]
- Quick Studies [IT]
- Snare Drum Improvisation [IT] – [VST]
- Drumset Improvisation [IT] – [VST]
- Drumset Composition [VST] – [MT]
- Solo Repertoire [MT] – [VLT]
- Chamber Music Repertoire [MT] – [VLT]

Some activities will be achieved after a very short time whereas others will require longer. Moreover, after some activities have been attained, a maintenance programme will be necessary: this is true for some technical exercises, rudiments, and some selected études and repertoire pieces, etc.

---

[3] *Transitional areas of correlation between Musicianship and Instrumental Development*

INTRODUCTION

Snare Drum Development (SDD) and Drum Set Development (DD) are, throughout the PercMP Development Areas, the main framework around which all other Development Areas orbit; these areas have been conceived to help percussion and drum teachers achieve a profound view of their student's improvements while guiding them throughout the higher levels of drum playing.

The student, while studying DD, should be simultaneously working on SDD: the level of DD tackled, should be one less than SDD's thus, when beginning the third level of SDD, the level of DD expressed in this book can be introduced.

As progress is made, a new Development Area may be added: the more areas the student manages, the more profoundly competence and skills will grow; nonetheless, SDD and DD should be the only Development Areas on which the student will be working constantly.

DD consists of short pieces that the student will have to prepare for the following lesson; how these pieces will be mastered is an issue to be pre-emptively clarified in order to positively monitor the student's progress. Therefore, the teacher will have to determine in advance which criteria to adopt when evaluating each piece and assigning a new one in its place.

The general complexity expressed at each level of DD does not have to be comparable to the difficulty of other areas simultaneously studied, especially if related to repertoire. Indeed, the student may find him/herself studying a repertoire piece that is much more difficult than is expressed by the level required in DD: this would be perfectly appropriate while the contrary would surely be unfitting. The time term of DD is classified as VST while a repertoire piece may be classified from MT to VLT; therefore, the latter can be more complex.

In the pieces throughout all levels of DD, rhythmic patterns and time signatures are gradually introduced: technical skills, rhythmic skills and a sense of meter will therefore gradually improve.

When composing these works, one of the main objectives was to supply both students and teachers with pieces in which the formal structures would well be identifiable, thus stimulating an attitude to analysing the pieces before studying them. Developing the ability to identify periods, phrases and motifs will surely allow the student to achieve a higher level of awareness; consequently, a higher degree of motivation for increasing one's technical skills will strongly improve. While performing these pieces the student will therefore not find him/herself playing a series of grooves, where a rhythmic motif or phrase is constantly repeated throughout the piece, but will be required to interpret, by considering the drum set as a solo instrument, pieces with a musical meaning in their whole, even though they may - at a very first stage - be only of eight measures long.

Each chapter ends with some exercises identified by roman numerals: these are provided as warm-up exercises to be kept for as long as the student will be tackling the pieces included in the same chapter.

Using this Book

There is no strict way for using this book, which can be adopted according to various purposes. Nevertheless, its mayn purpose is that to be part of the Drum Set Development (DD) within the Percussion Method Project (PercMP). The teacher who wishes to follow the PercMP principles will here find the musical material conceived to develop an effective and comprehensive programme.

The Five Modes Approach

By having previously played the pieces from 'Snare Drum Development L2' (SDD), the student will be aware of the rhythmic patterns and time signatures involved in the pieces from this book. The adoption of the 'five mode approach'[1] as presented in SDD - proposed in order to favour a gradual approach for internalising the complexity of the pieces - will no longer be necessary.

Rhythm

The student will be required to interpret the following durations and rhythmic patterns, in addition of those introduced in the previous level:

---

1   The five modes approach, as presented in SDD:

In order to internalise these pieces we suggest five ways (named 'modes'), eventually among others, for practicing. Although not all may be required, when more than one is adopted, they should be studied according to the following order:

Mode 1: The student claps the rhythm while pronouncing the rhythm-syllables or counting out loudly. At this stage, the student should perform at a tempo suitable for comfortably clapping the fastest rhythmic patterns within the piece, thus not necessarily at the required tempo.

Mode 2: The student performs the rhythm by gently tapping on his/her thighs, respecting R & L indications, while simultaneously pronouncing the rhythm-syllables or counting out loudly.

Mode 3: While using a damper with the snares disengaged, the student plays with the drumsticks respecting R & L indications, while simultaneously pronouncing the rhythmic syllables, or counting out loudly.

Mode 4: With the snares engaged and the use of drumsticks the student will play respecting R & L indications, while mentally-pronouncing the rhythm-syllables or counting .

Mode 5: The student performs like as in mode 4 while the teacher improvises a second part. The improvised part can be a counter-rhytmic part played on another drum or set of drums, a piece played on another instrument or sung, and so forth.

Binary Durations

Ternary Durations and Patterns

At this level – in addition to those introduced in the previous level – the following time signatures will be found:

$\frac{7}{4} \quad \frac{3}{8} \quad \frac{9}{8} \quad \frac{5}{8} \quad \frac{7}{8}$

Set of instruments for this level, R & L indications, Note Reading

At this level, the set needed requires three instruments: a snare drum, a ride cymbal and a floor tom, notated on the staff as shown in Fig. 1.

Fig. 1

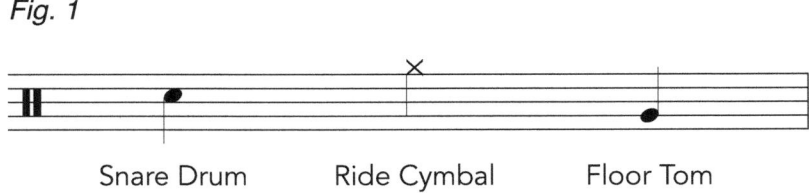

Snare Drum   Ride Cymbal   Floor Tom

Hands indications – also known as 'sticking' – are specified with R and L signs, considering the snare drum placed between the player's knees, the ride cymbal placed on the player's right side, slightly forward, and the floor tom placed on the player's right side. When opting to placing the instruments in a different way, the R & L signs should be revised acoordingly. We encourage to strictly follow these indications, indeed conceived to develop, in a balanced way, the student's right and left side; consequently, there is no left or right-handedness propensity throughout this and other levels. Some pieces will require the use of diddles while others will develop alternating single strokes.

A percussionist (as any other instrumentalist) should be able to sing at sight and read notated pitches fluently; to claim the contrary is a misconception that may lead to a limited improvement of the student's skills.

Styles

Styles are not introduced in this book, and may be studied together with repertoire, according to the programme adopted and the student's interest; in that context the student will deal with all the various rhythmic patterns, ostinatos, grooves, characteristic accentuations and other intrinsic elements typical to specific styles.

Metronome

Metronome marks mainly suggest at what pace a piece should be played; in some cases the metronome's mark value is expressed by two numbers indicating a range in which the piece's pace should fall. Playing with a metronome is a task much more difficult than what it may not seem; it may be more productive to play duets in order to practice a fluent and uniform pace. When playing with a metronome, the student is required to constantly adjust his/her own pace to the metronome's beat while, when playing with another person, the adjustment is mutual.

Improvising Chamber Music

We encourage all teachers to improvise duets with their students as an alternative way of playing these and other pieces. Once the student is indeed able to play a piece from this series, improvising duets with another drum or set of drums will improve coordination, inner-hearing and motivation. Improvised duets may not only be performed with a second drum: any other available instrument, including the voice, may be used. Changing roles is also important: the teacher or another student can play the piece while the student improvises an accompaniment or any other rhythmic structure.

Some Teaching Directions

Each assigned piece should be prepared and fully mastered for the next lesson (usually the following week).

The student, when practacing, should be able to solve all problems related to the preparation of the piece, know how to interpret all involved rhythmic patterns, durations and time signatures included therein; consequently the student should be able, by practicing along the period within the following lesson, to perform the piece with a high degree of competence.

Moving to a New Piece

When evaluating if a piece has to be considered mastered and therefore archived and replaced by another one, a set of criterions should be considered as evaluating parameters. According to each student's poise, level of musicianship, general aptitude and so forth, more or less criterions may be considered.

Main, mandatory criterions could be:

- The piece must be played with a flow and no interruption
- Rhythms and durations must be accurate
- R & L indications must be respected
- The tempo may not be accurate as indicated, although the mood and the tempo itself should be appropriate to the piece's character

Further criterions that may apply according to the teacher's discretion, could be, among others:

- Playing should be realized in a relaxed and anxiousless way
- Hairpins diminuendos should be respected
- Dynamics and crescendo hairpins should be respected
- Articulation and accent signs should be respected
- Phrasing and a sense of the meter should be expressed
- The required grip should be controlled throughout the piece

Once established, the criterions chosen for evaluating all performances must be strictly maintained throughout the level; if the student's performance don't meet the teacher's criterions the piece should be maintained as an objective for the next lesson; when the performance meets the established criterions for a positive evaluation, the piece will be archived and replaced by a following one within the same level.

Before beginning this book the student should already have played the first few pieces from Snare Drum Development L3, thus starting Drum Set Development from a level previous than the one selected for SDD. The student will therefore be simultaneously working on two levels: one from

SDD and one from DD. The teacher should assign at least one piece from each area (SDD and DD) taking care to complete the two levels almost at the same time.

The overall quantity of pieces from the two levels of SDD and DD weekly assigned should be:

DD and SDD Weekly Assigned Work (total no. of pieces)				
Task Type	*Pieces from SDD*	*Pieces from DD*	*Total Pieces Assigned*	*Pieces Evaluated Weekly*
Light	1 or 2	1	2 or 3	1 or 2
Medium	3	1 or 2	4 or 5	2 or 3
Intense	4 or 5	2 or 3	6 to 8	4 to 6
Demanding	6	3 or 4	9 or 10	7 to 8

It is important to not evaluate all assigned pieces at each lesson: as a consequence, the non-played pieces will settle within the time before the next lesson; this is an important issue due to the fact that non all the pieces may be well prepared for every following lesson, and for different reasons, not always dependent on the student's diligence.

Four or five total pieces are quite an important task to deal within a weak's work, considering that each lesson will include activities from other areas as well; we therefore recommend to assign this quantity of pieces, chategorized as a medium task, as it can be seen in the above table.

Monitoring

The teacher should keep a detailed record of all activities carried out at each lesson; this will provide an important amount of data that will make the teacher aware of the student's progress and improvements.

Although the teacher may select and assign a new piece according to a personal order, it is important to study a new piece following their numeric order. This book is divided in chapters, each of which deals with a single - up to a few - specific details. The student may be studying one or more pieces from two consecutive chapters.

Although all pieces will never be of the exact same level of difficulty, they are indeed conceived to meet characteristics that will distinguish them to be part of the specific level defined by this book.

LIST OF ABBREVIATIONS

MusMP: Music Method Project

MMP: Musicianship Method Project

PercMP: Percussion Method Project

SDD: Snare Drum Development

DD: Drum Set Development

LH: Left hand

RH: Right hand

Development Area: in PercMP each area is a branch, a sectors in which specific skills are developed.

Activity[2]: it can be a piece, an exercise, anything from a one bar rhythm to a whole movement of a much more complex composition, provided that it is a whole defined item. An activity is part of a specific Development Area.

Objective: it's a specific task and intended to be accomplished according to a predetermined period of time. An objective is a part or can coincide with an entire activity.

Duration[3]: any rhythmic value that coincides with the pulse value or any multiple of that value.

Rhythmic pattern: a sequence of rhythmic values usually smaller than the pulse value and perceived as a structure generally fitting one[4] beat duration.

---

2   As an example, a thirty-two bar piece is divided in two sections of sixteen bars each: only one section is required to be studied for the time arranged with the student. In this case the whole piece is the activity while the single section is the objective. Let's say that in addition to the piece's section, one rudiment and one study are also assigned: all of these are different objectives from activities from different development areas.

3   Duration also may refer to the lenght of time of a piece.

4   Rhythmic patterns may also fit multiple beat durations; the most common ones, however, fit one or two beats.

I

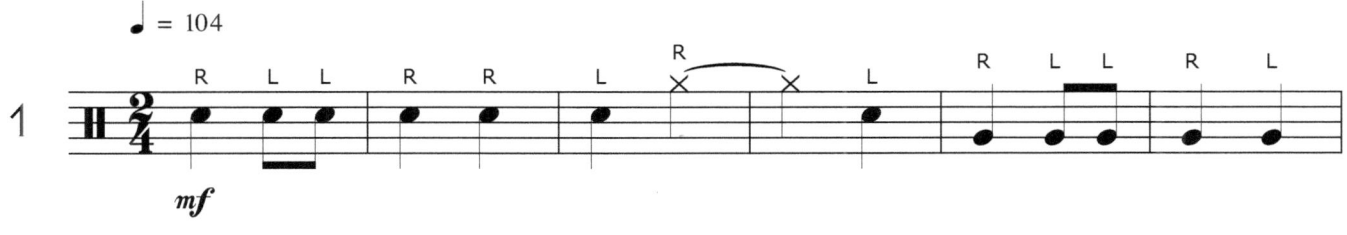

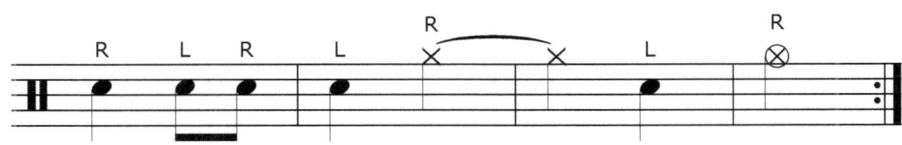

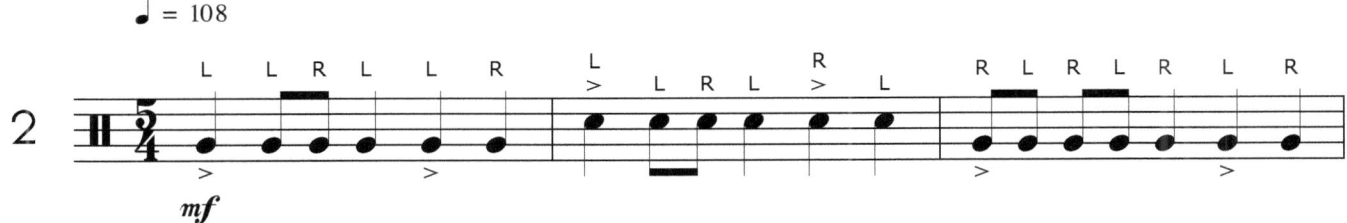
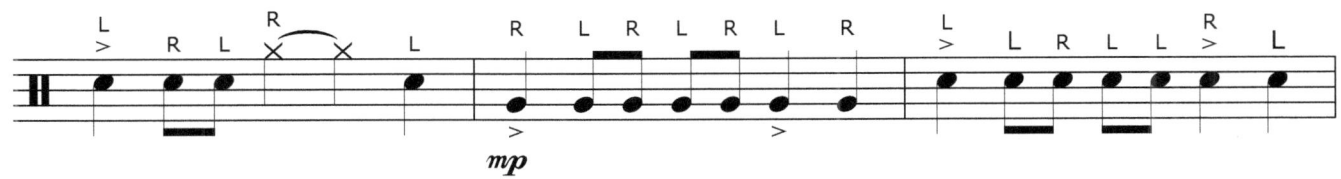
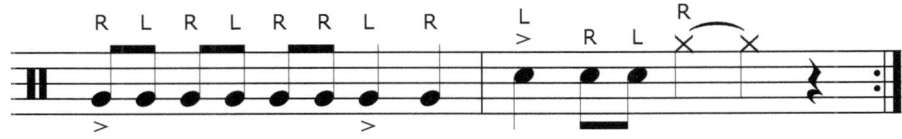

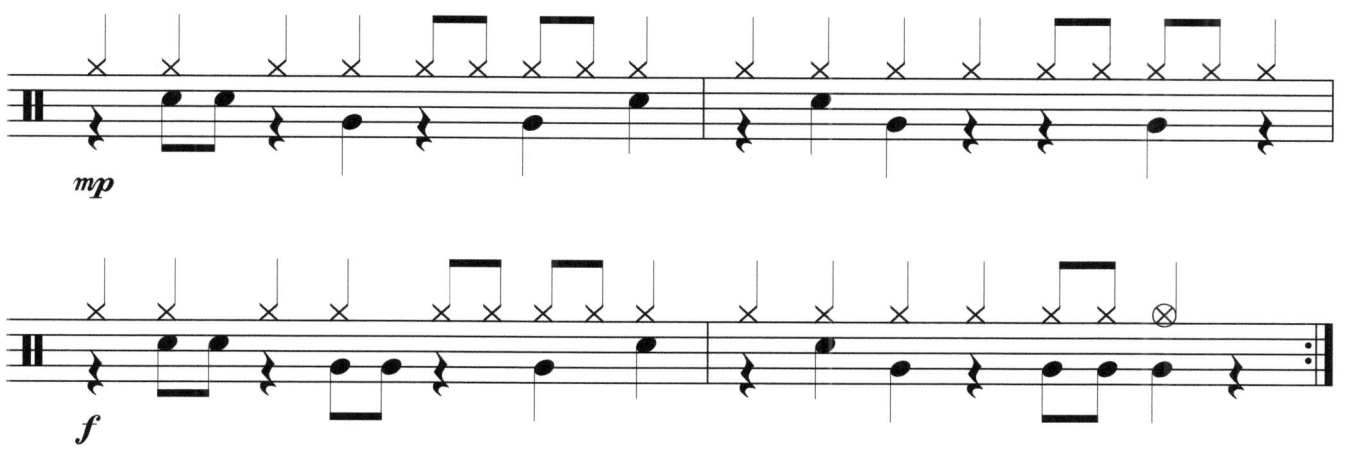

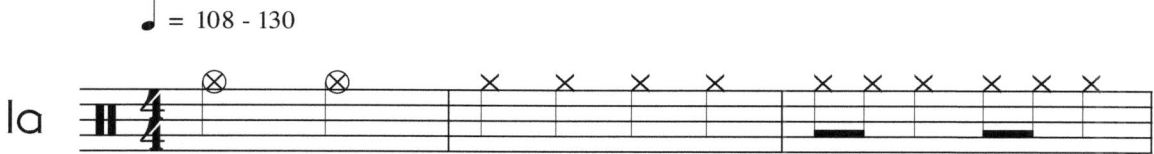

1a ♩ = 108 - 130

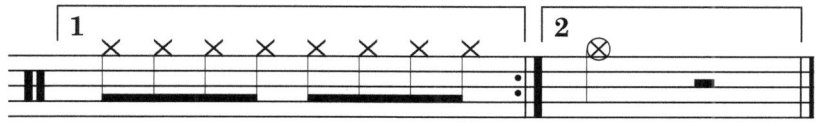

1b ♩ = 108 - 130

lc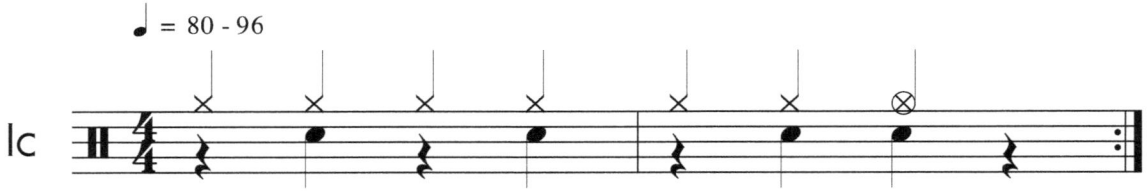

ld

le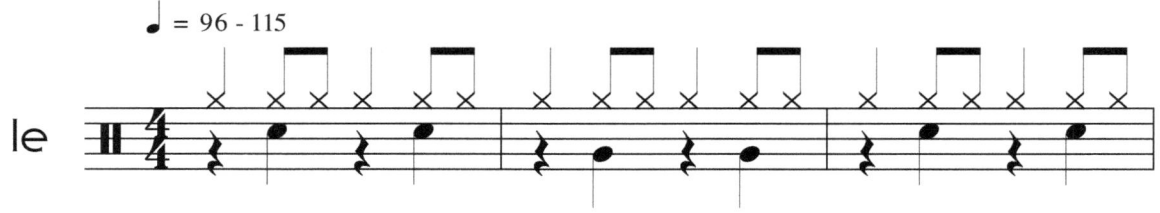

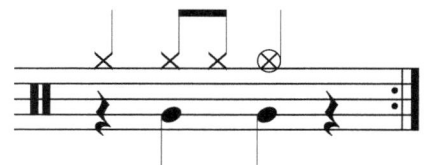

II

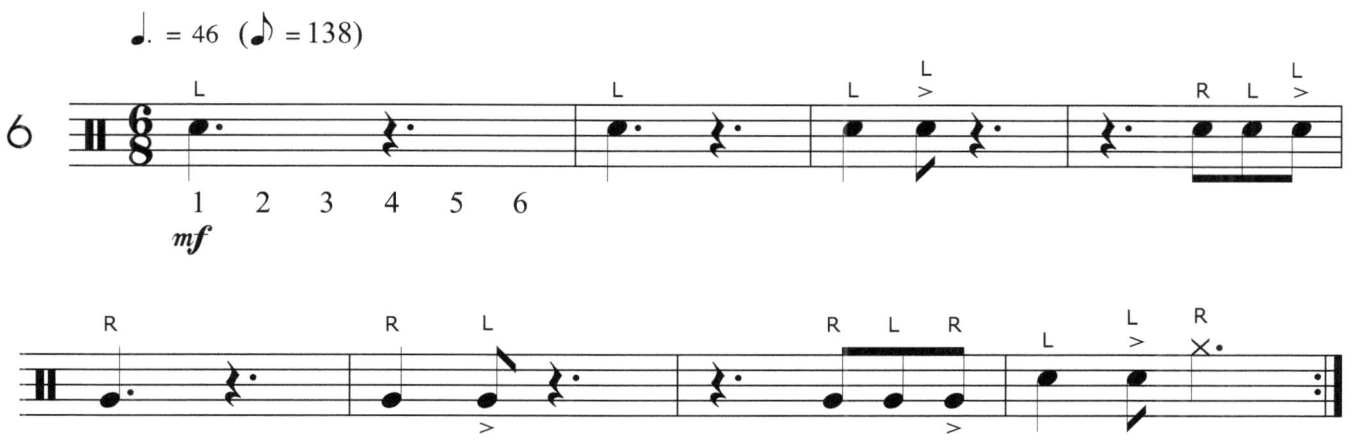

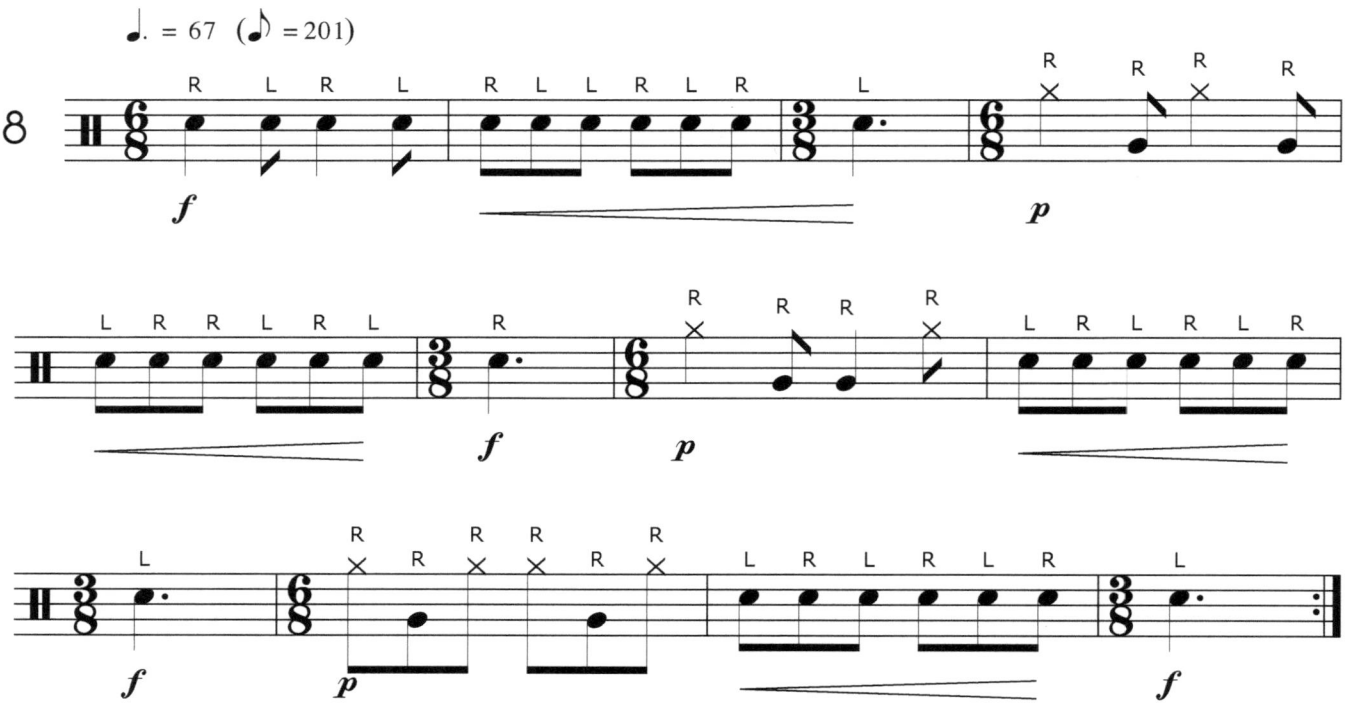

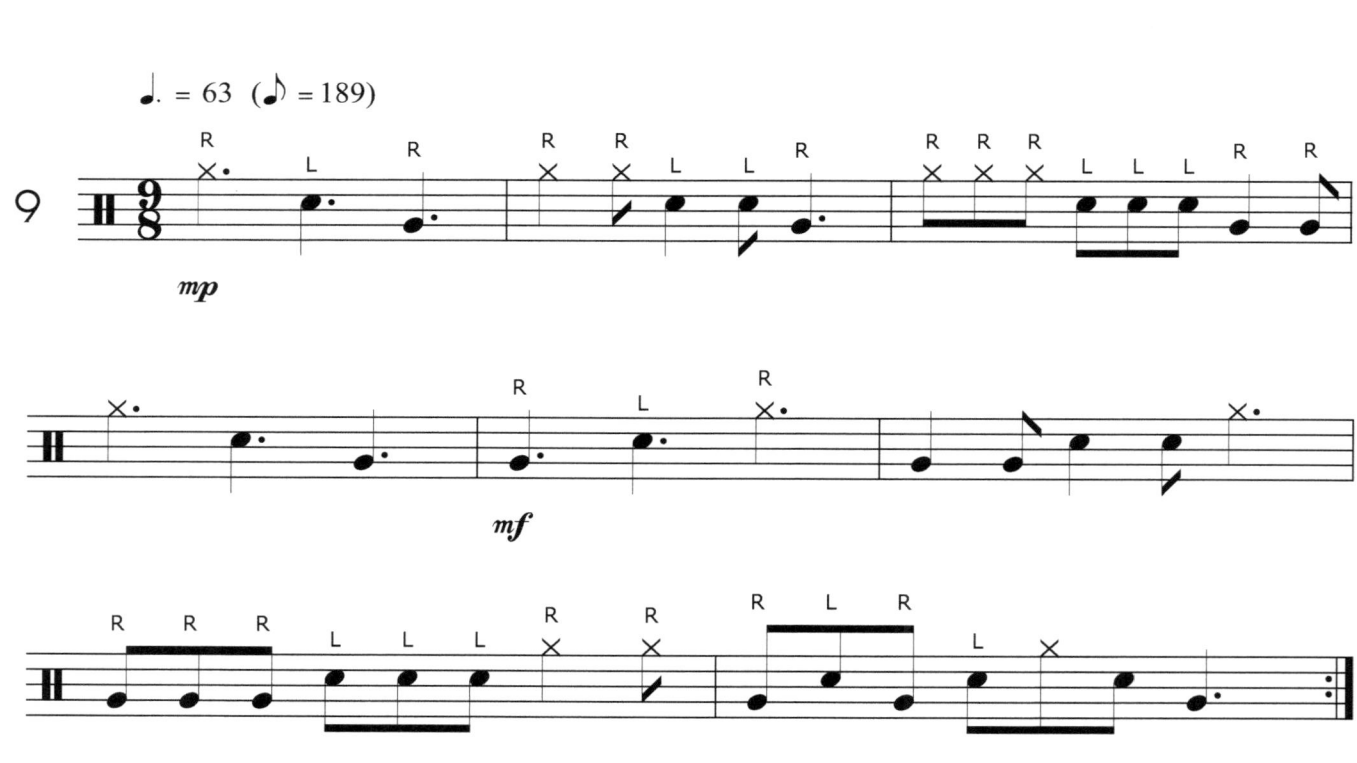

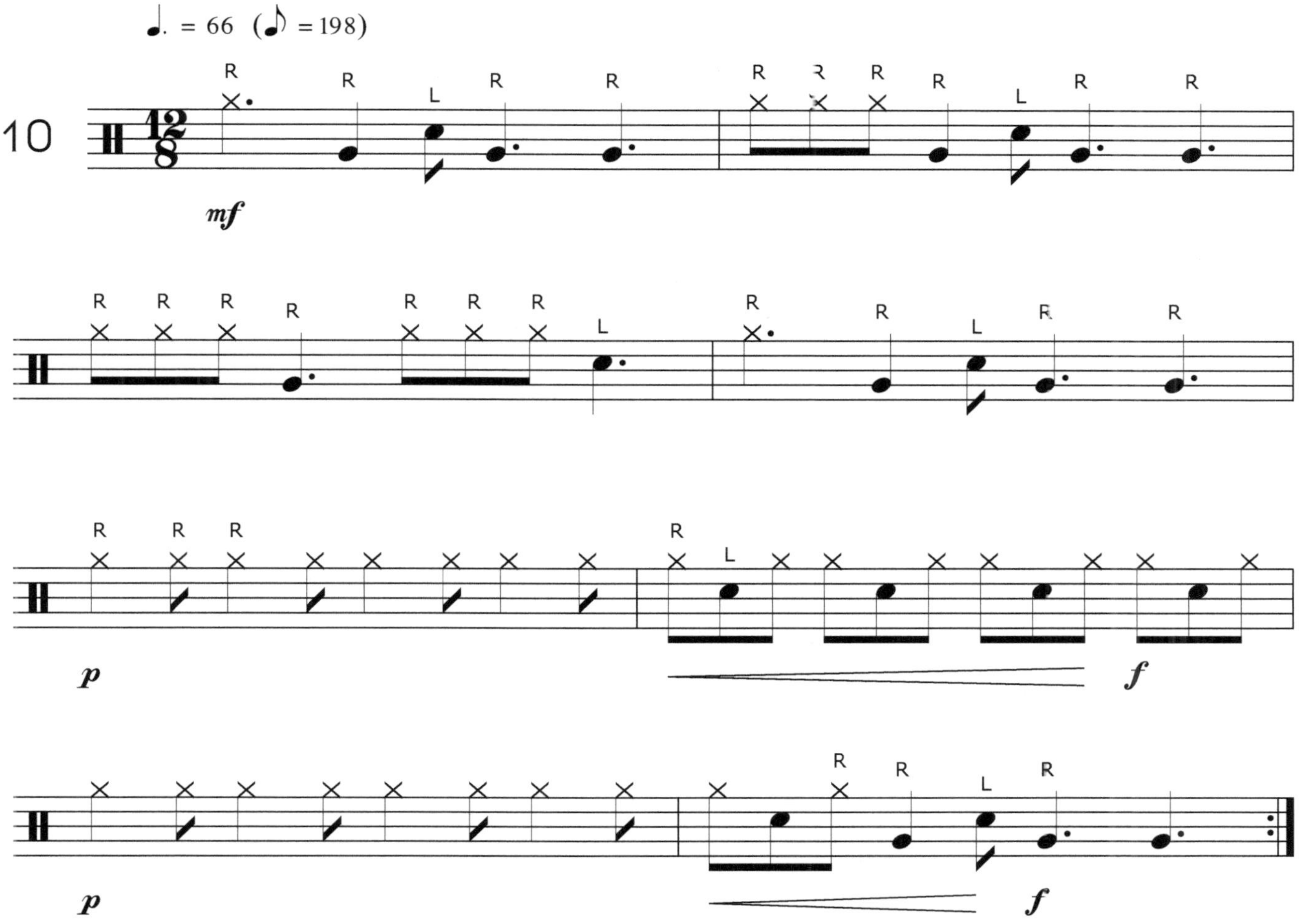

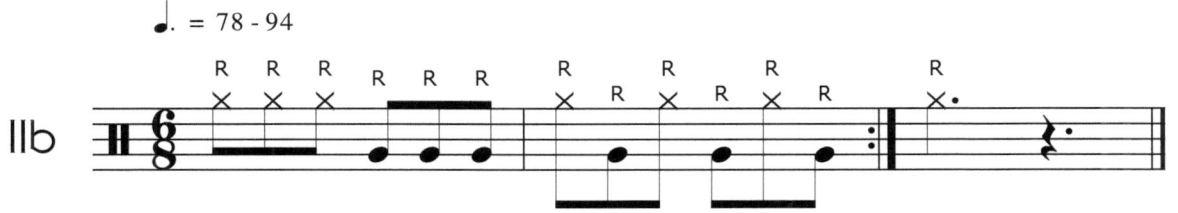

III

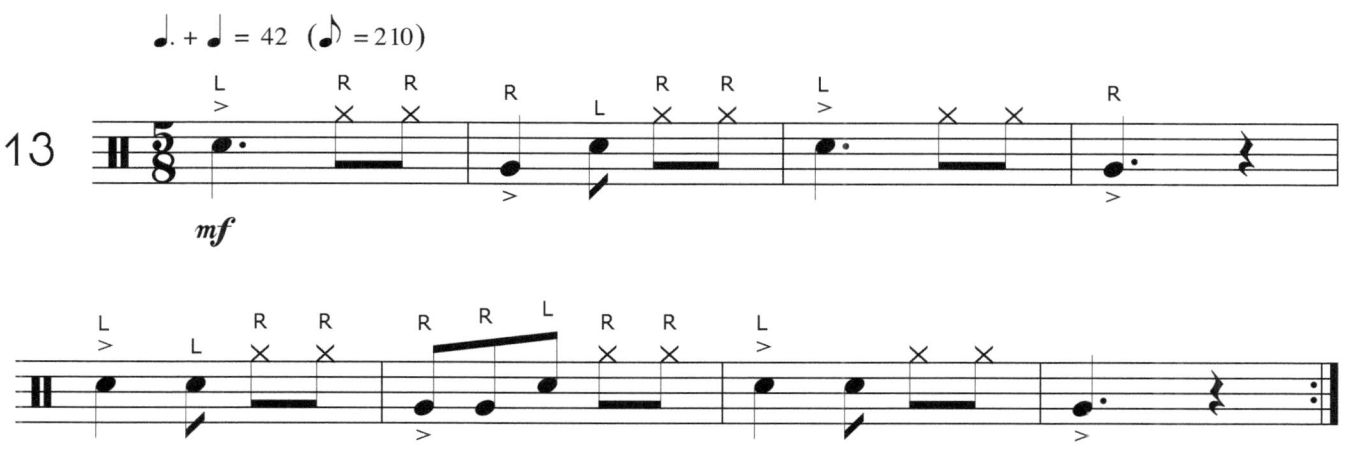
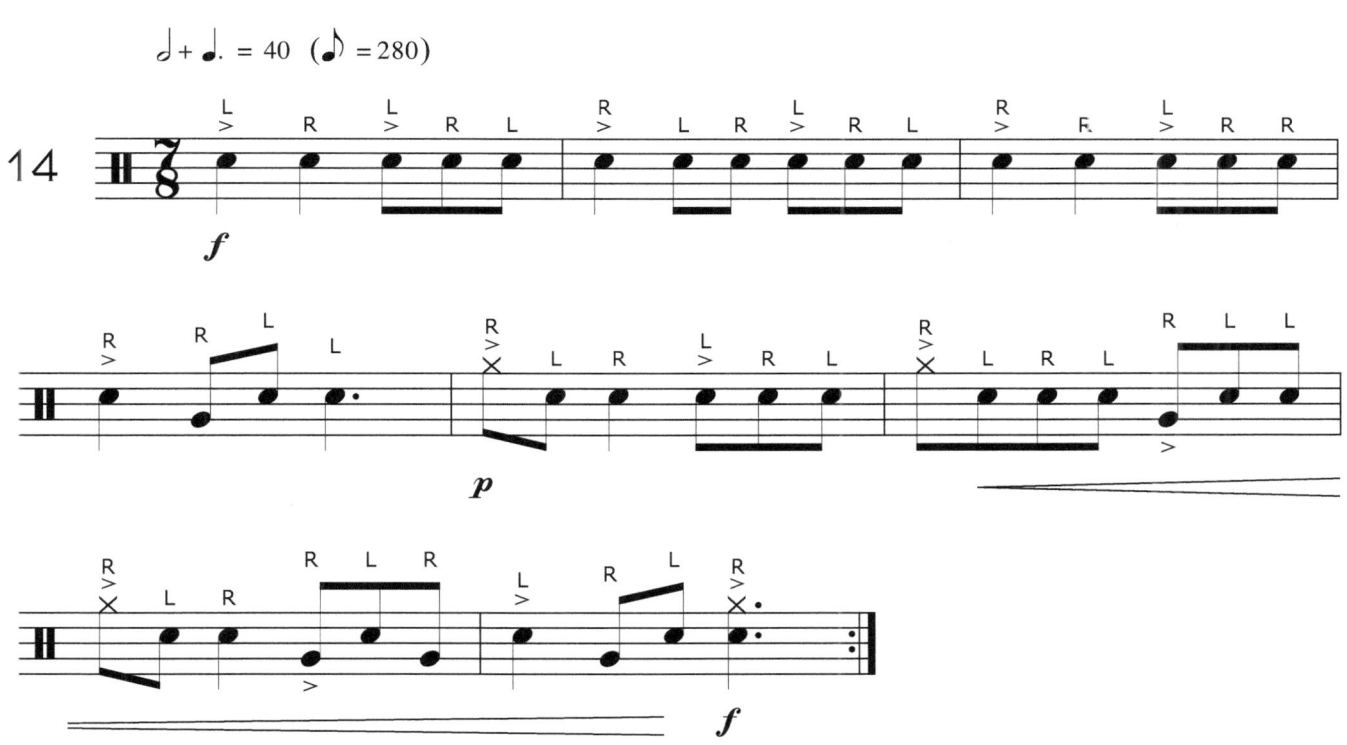

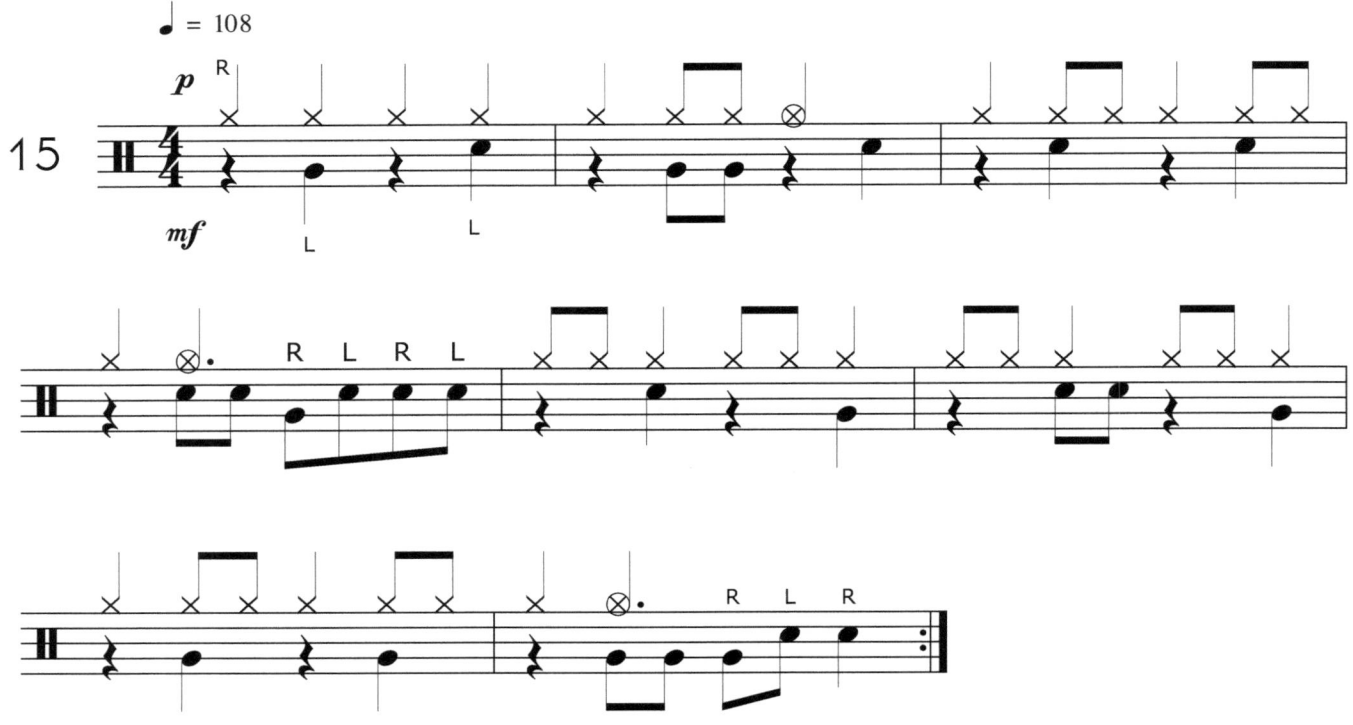

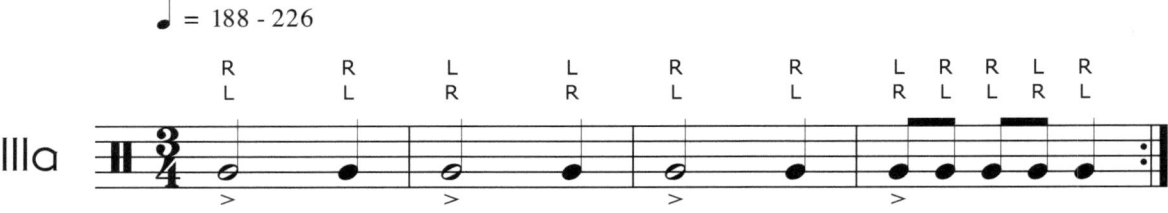

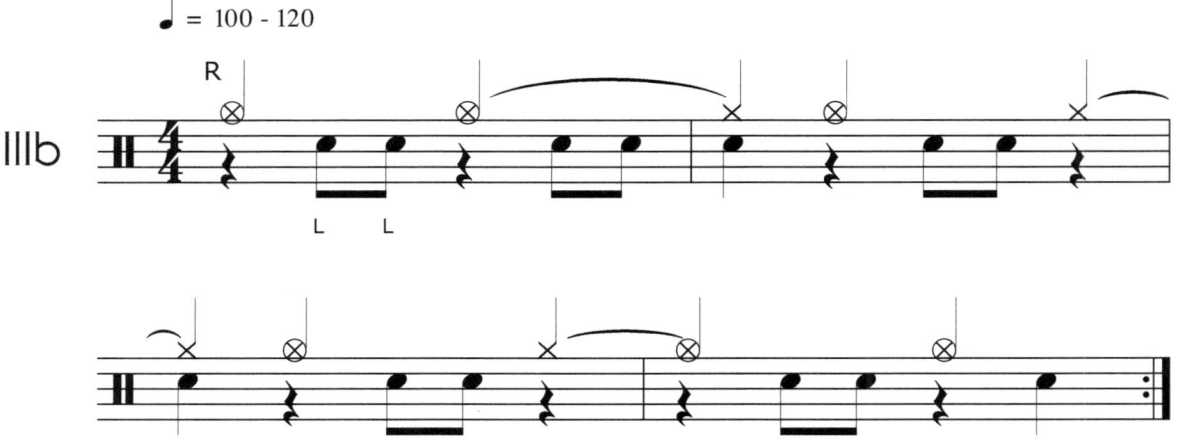

IV

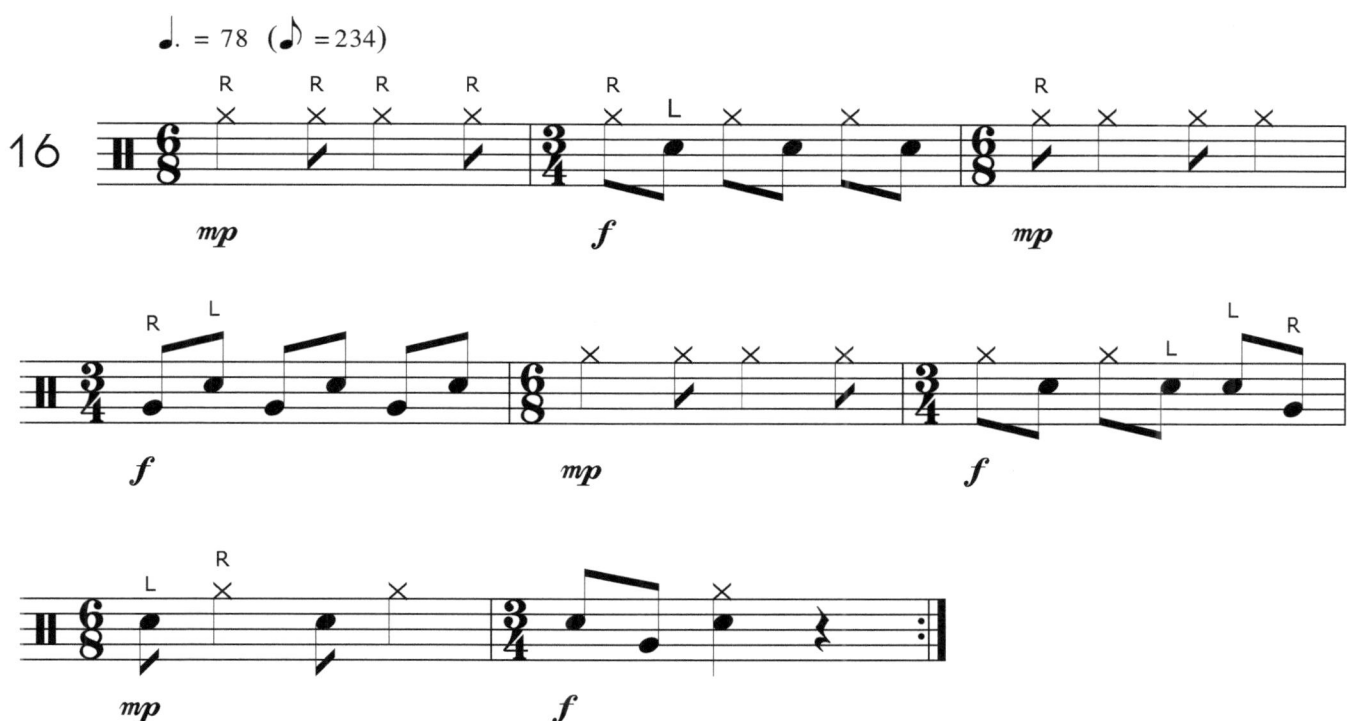

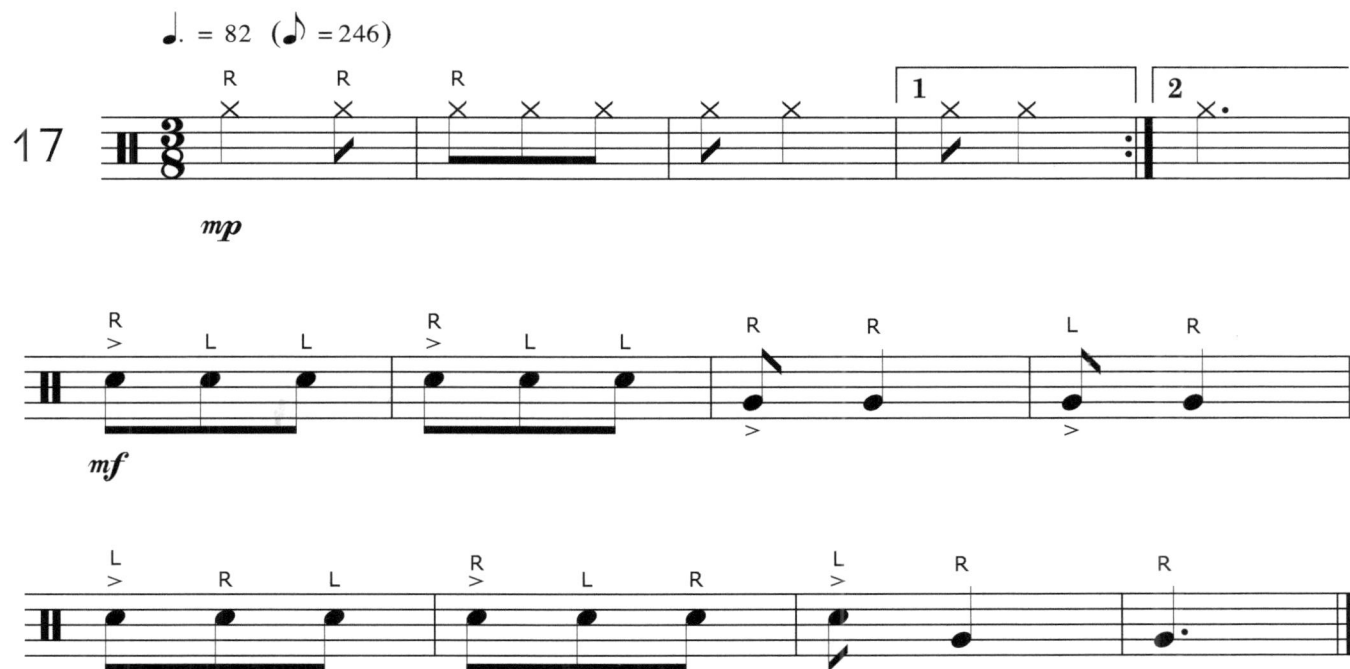

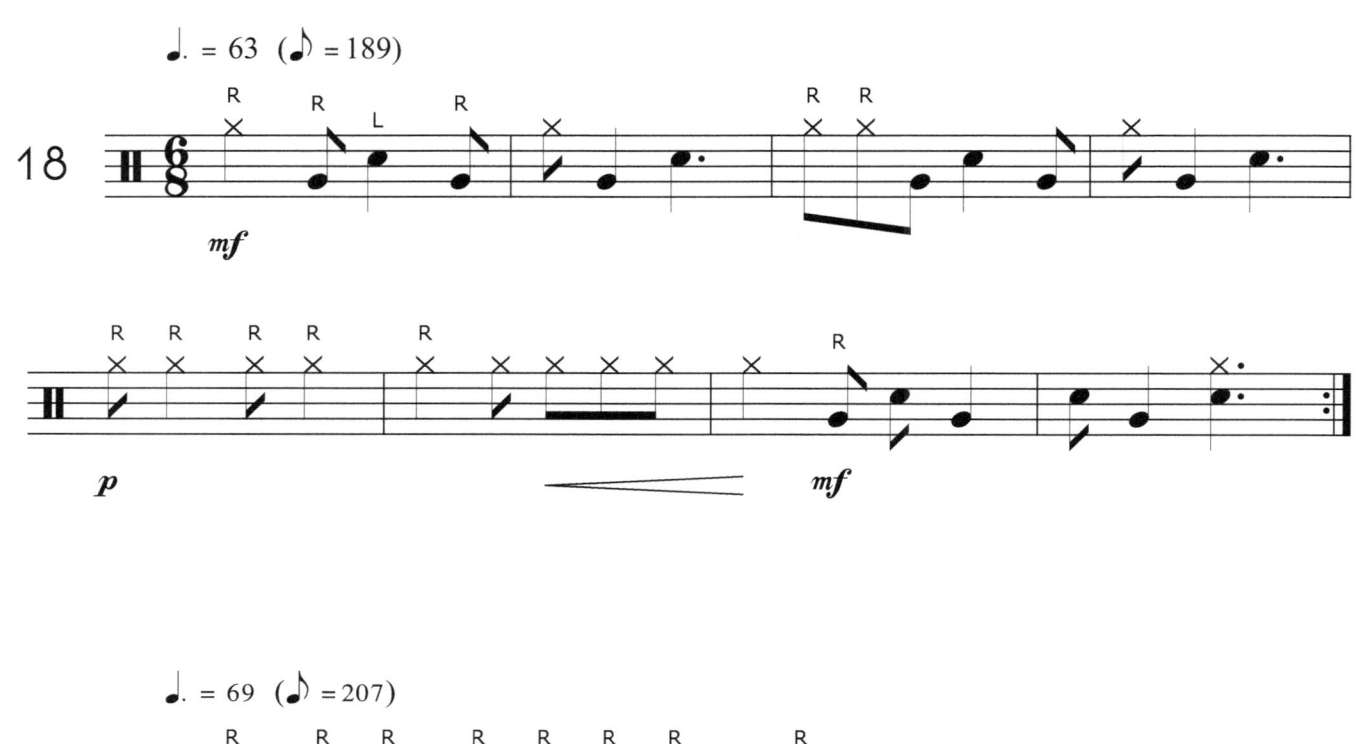

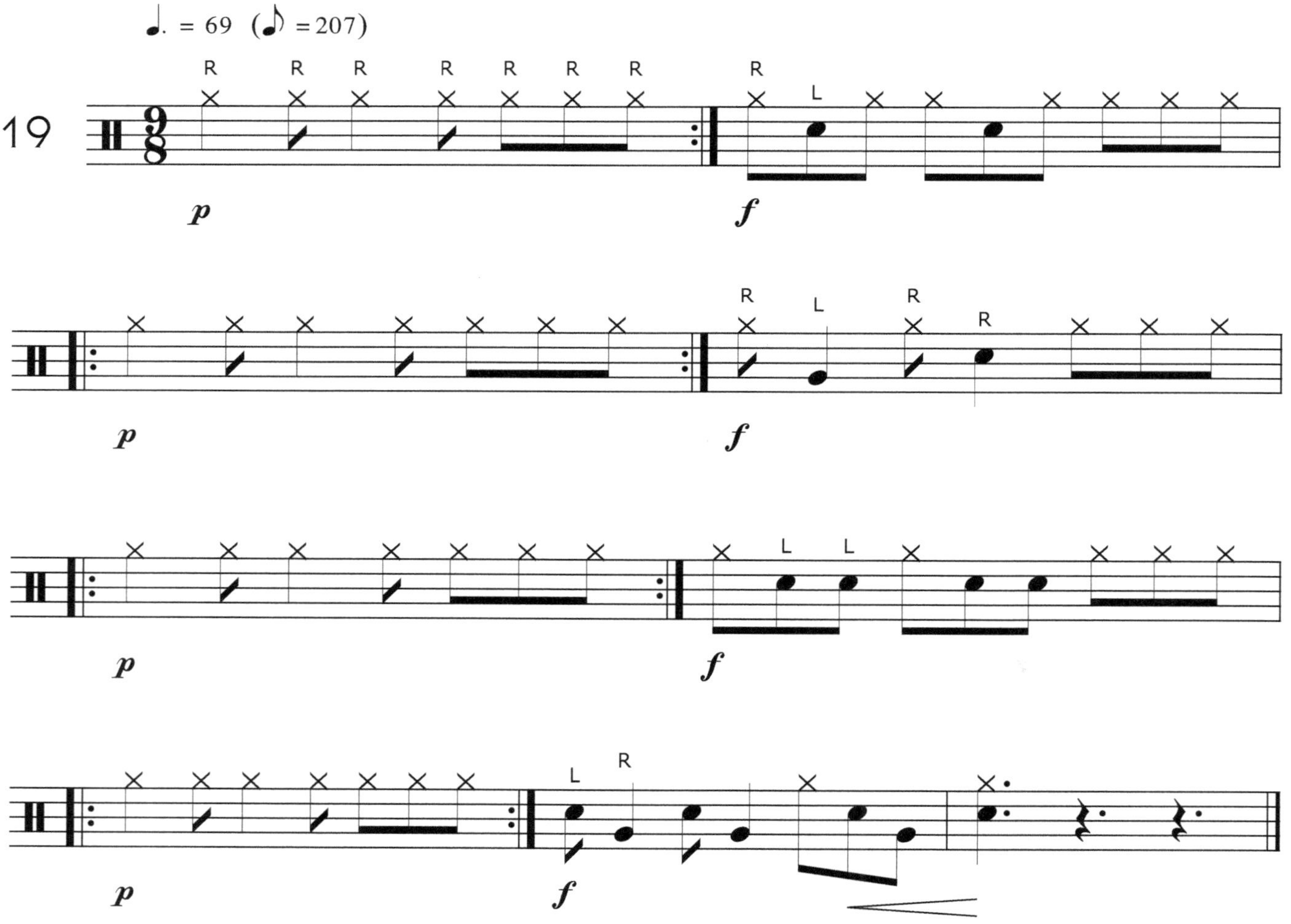

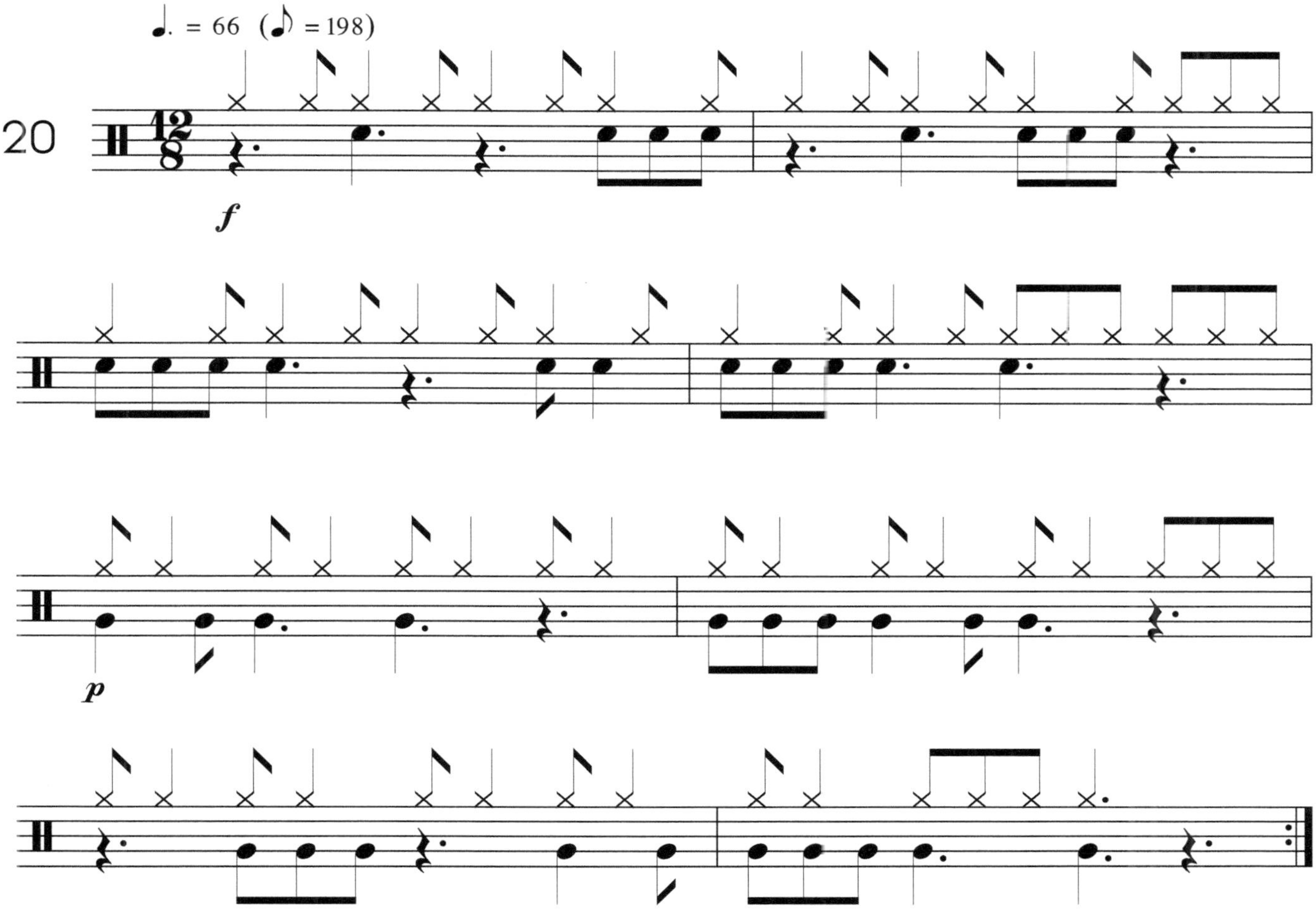

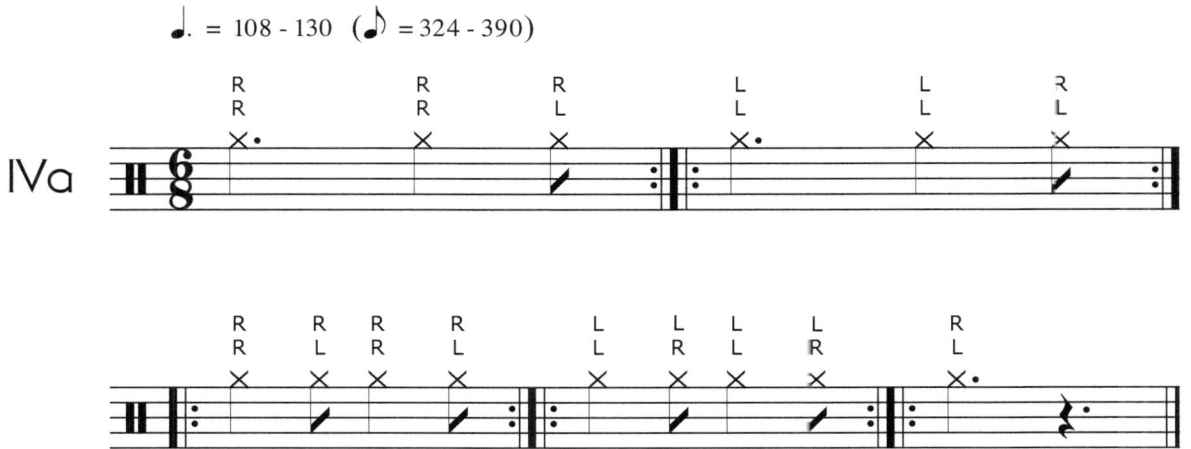

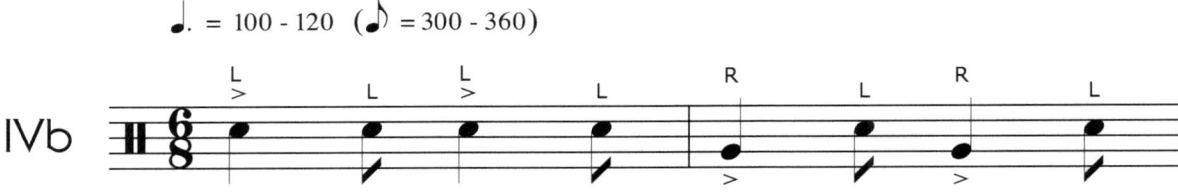

V

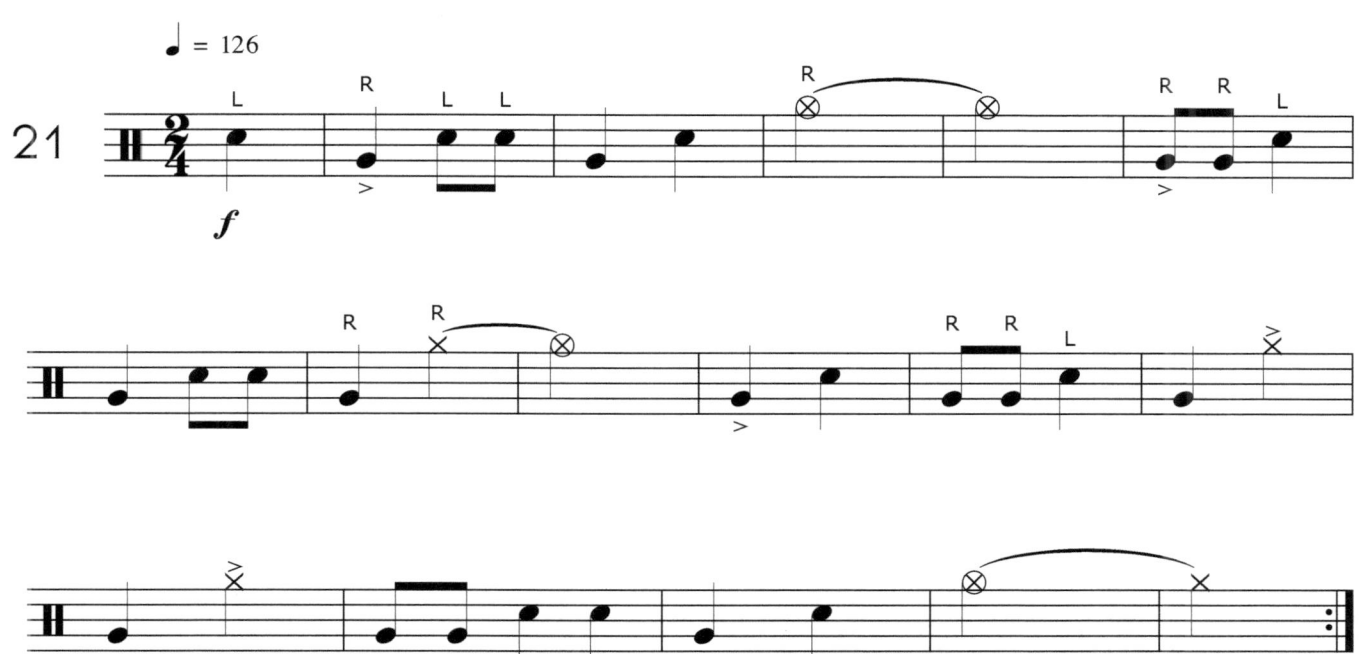

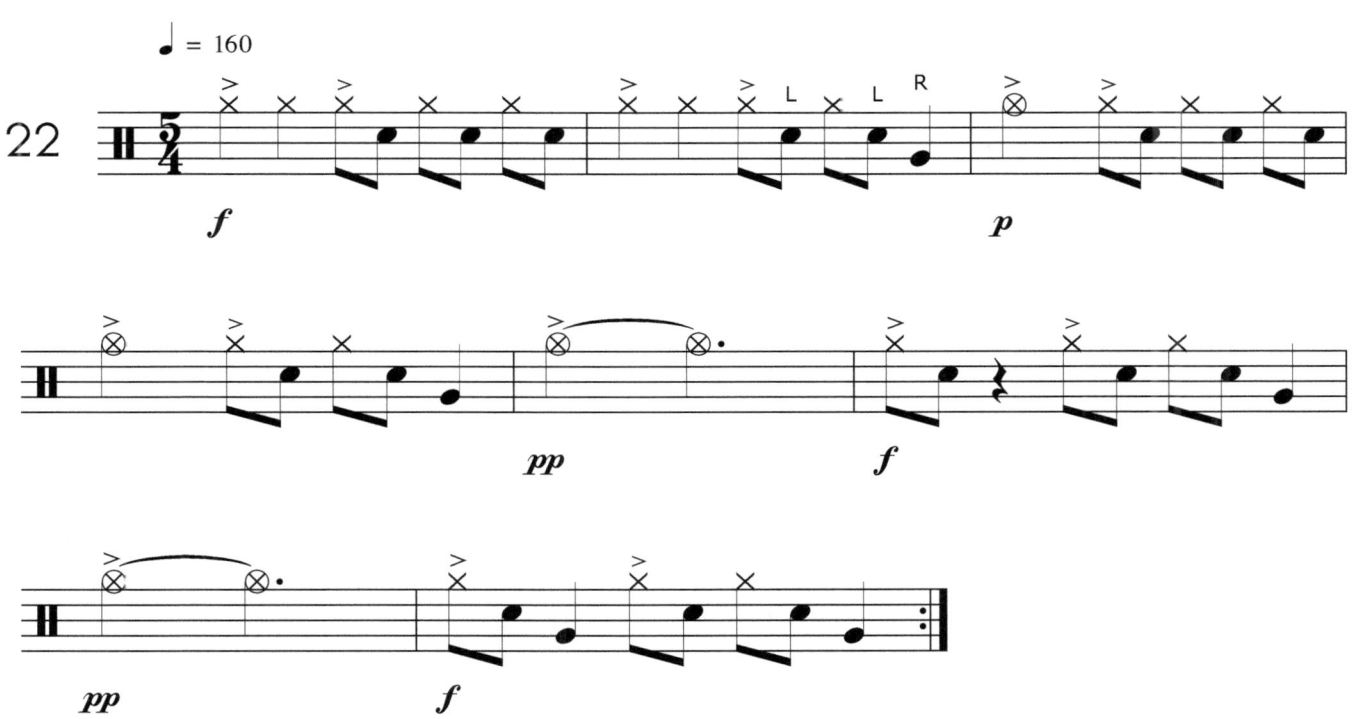

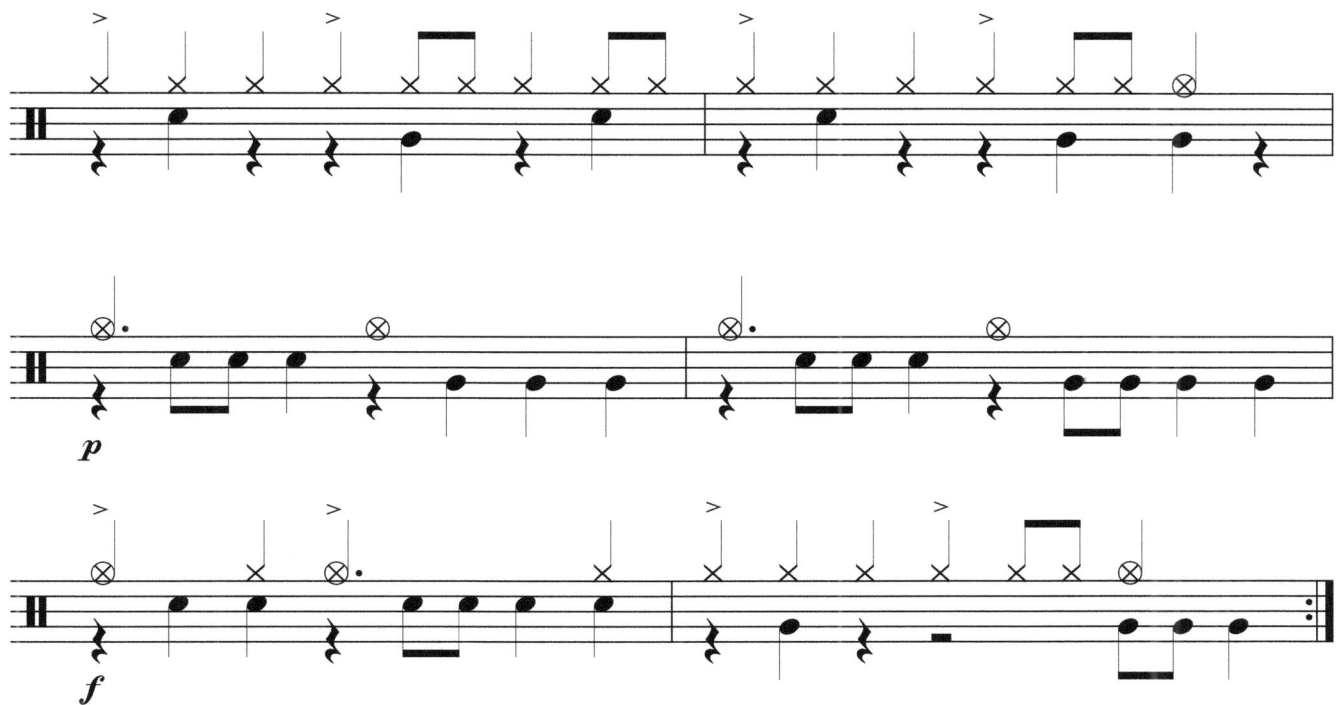

Va

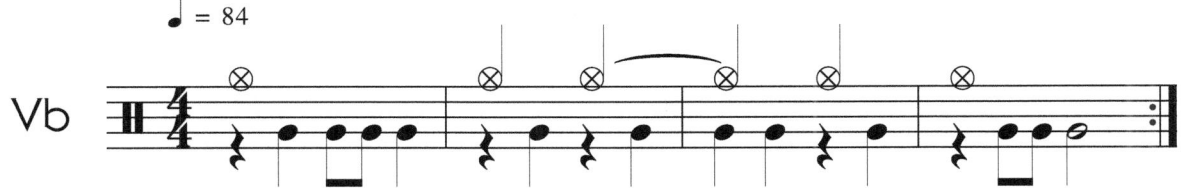

Vb

VI

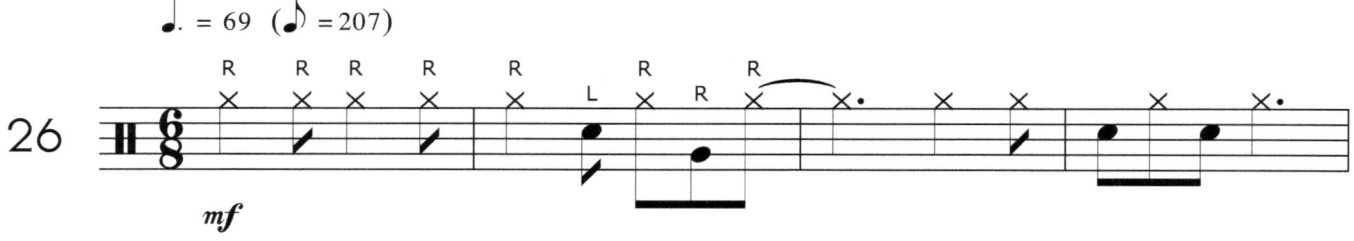
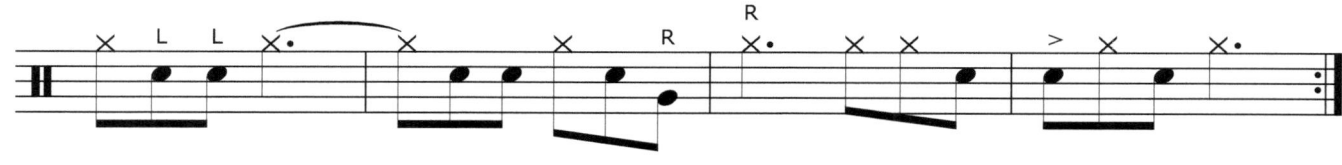
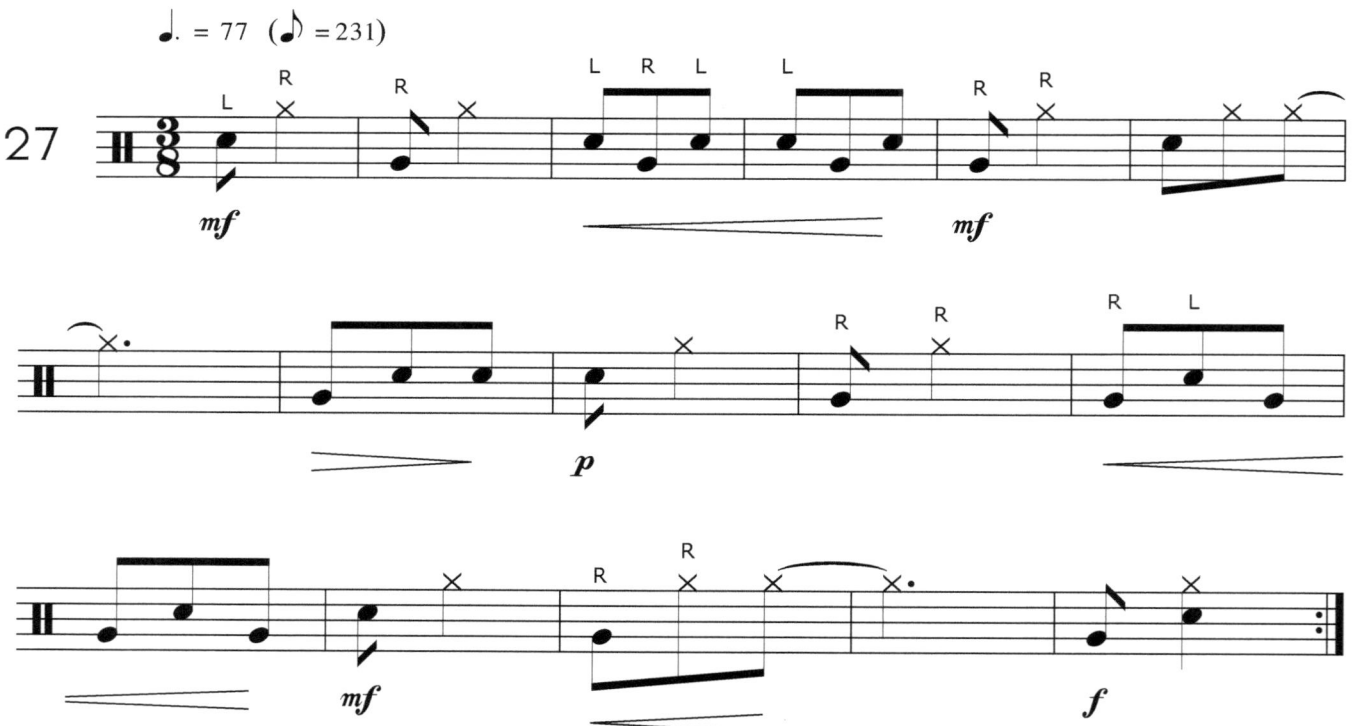

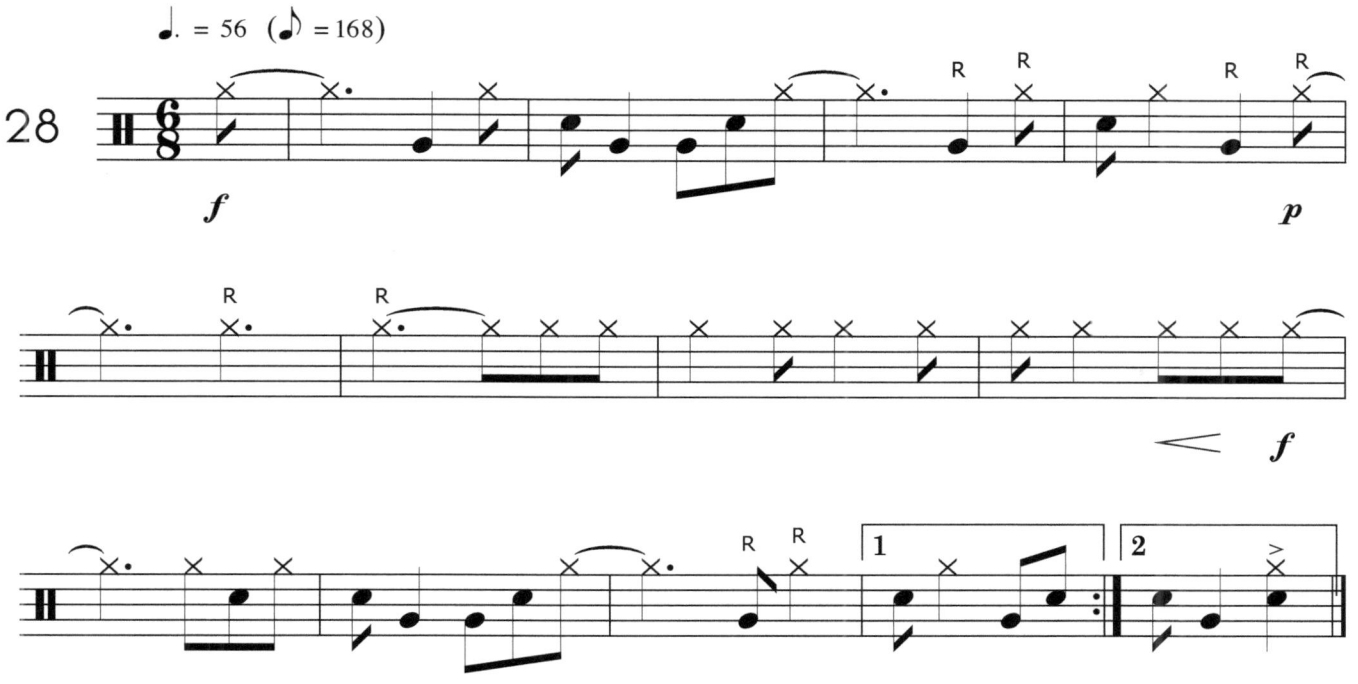
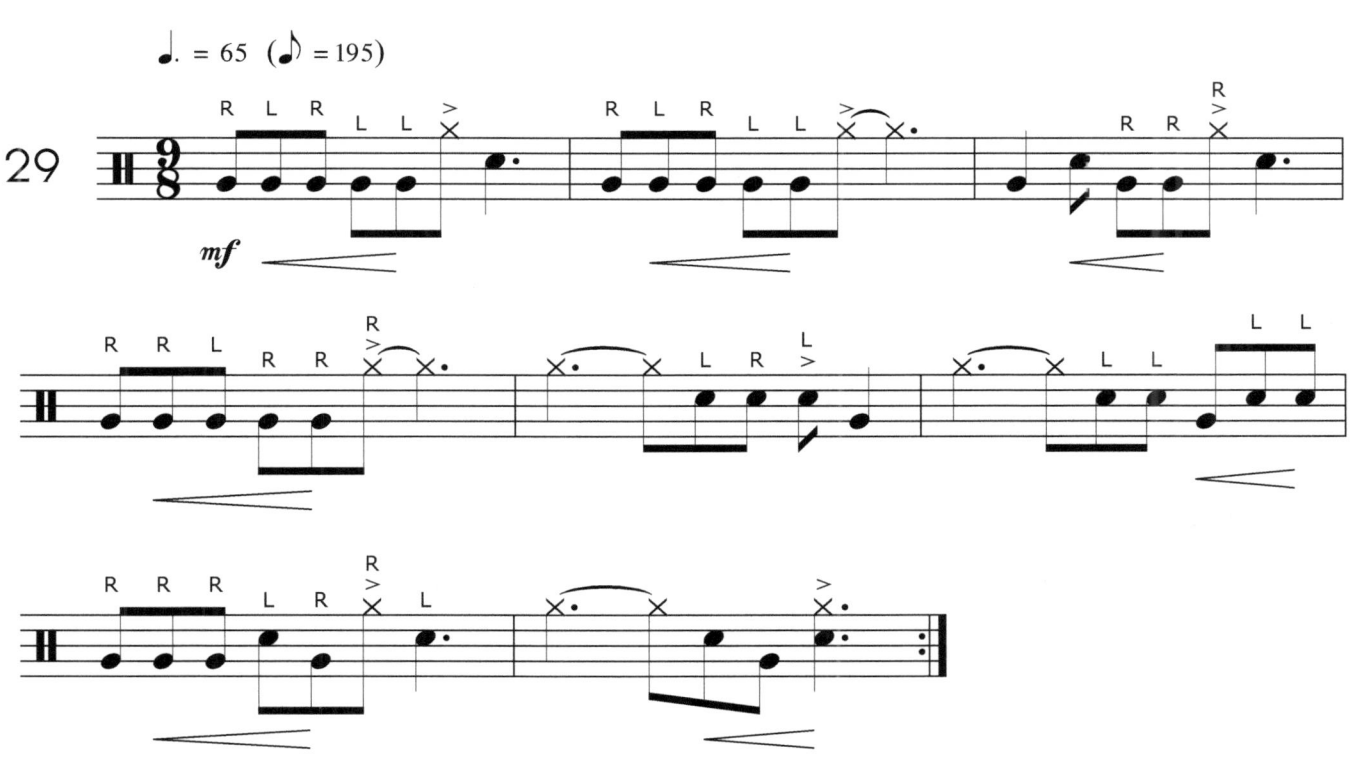

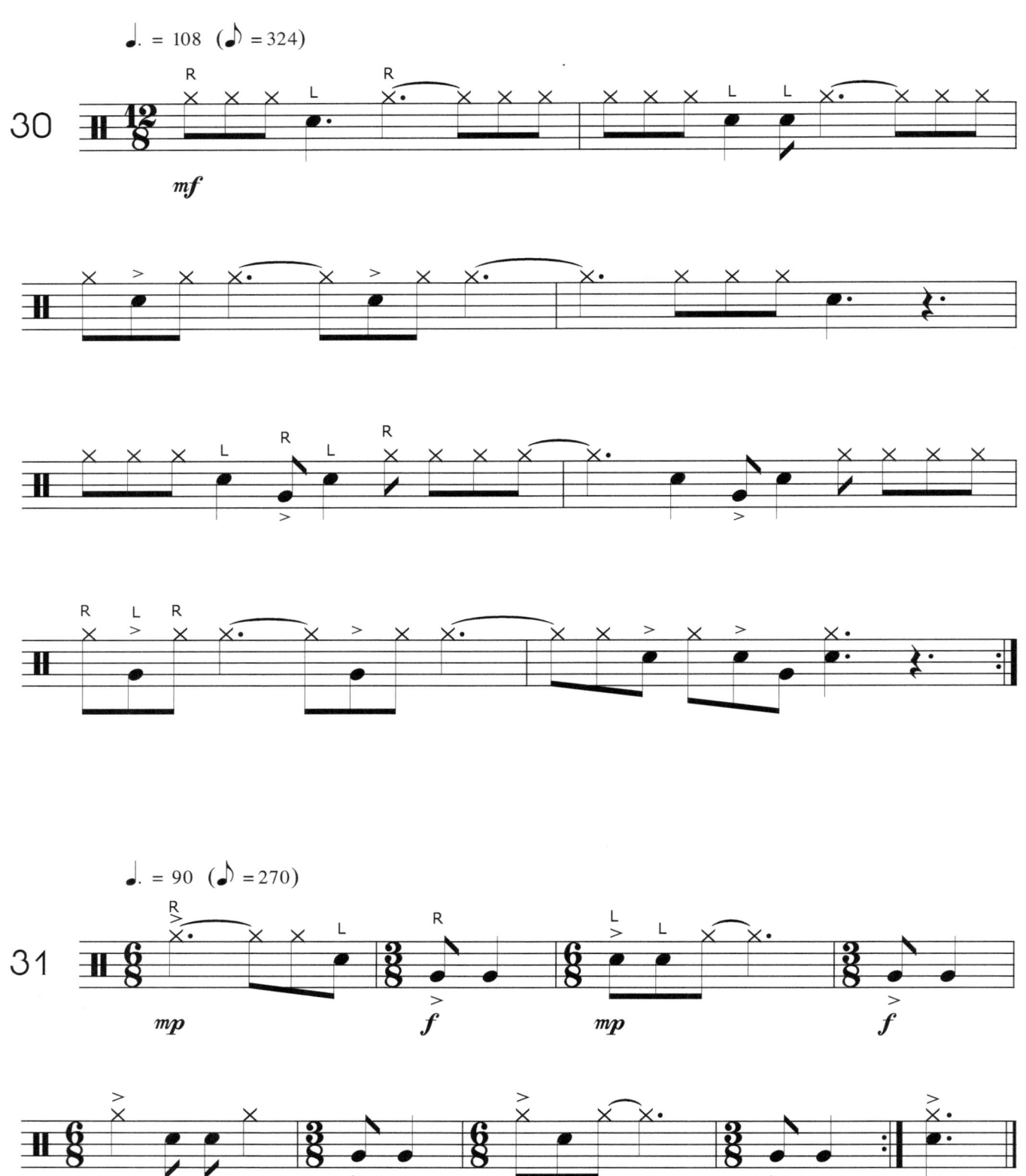

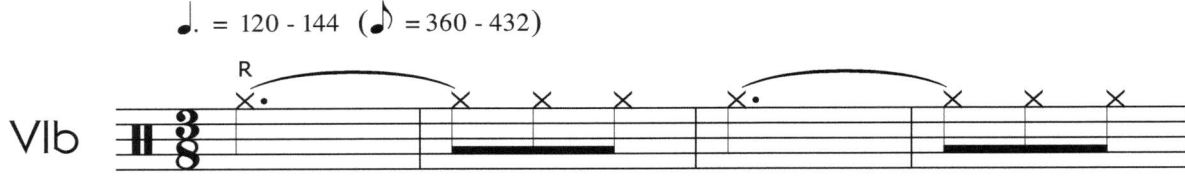

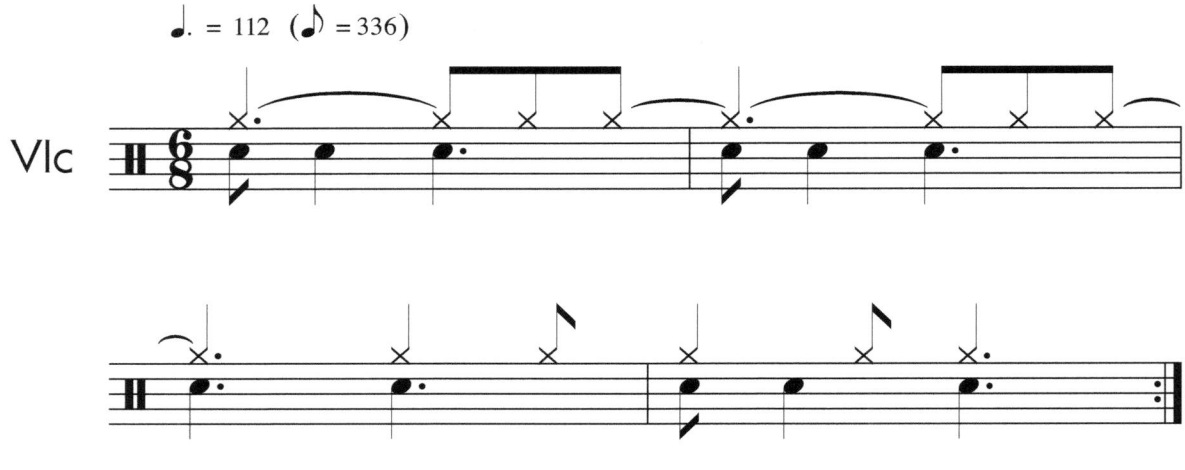

VII

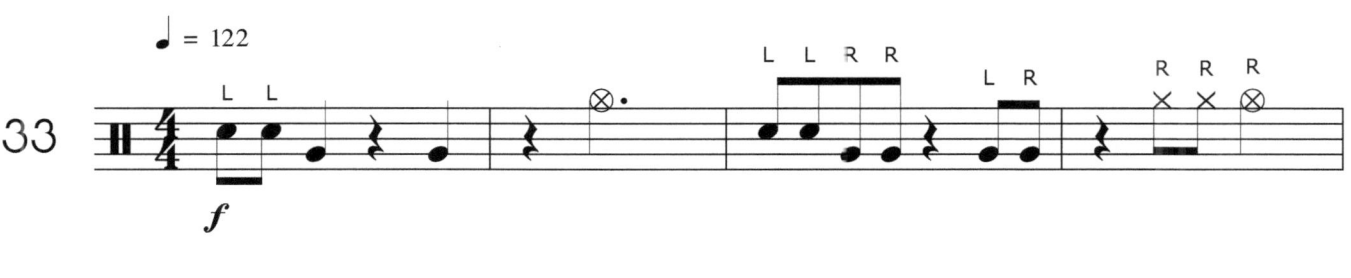

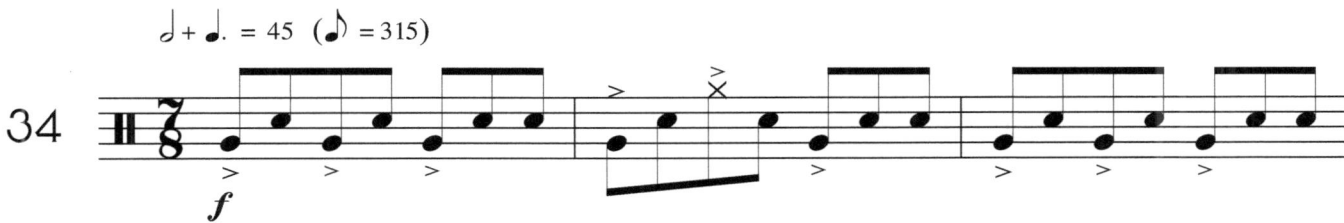
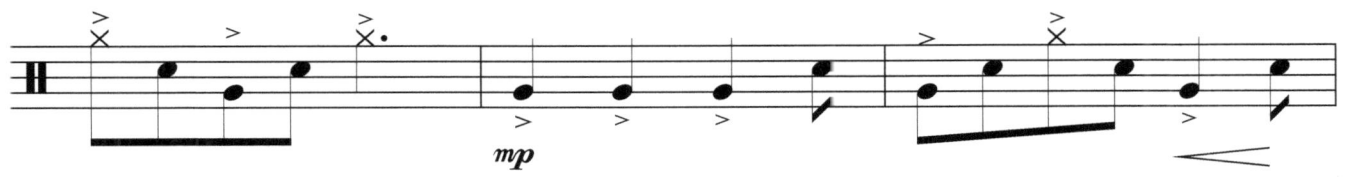

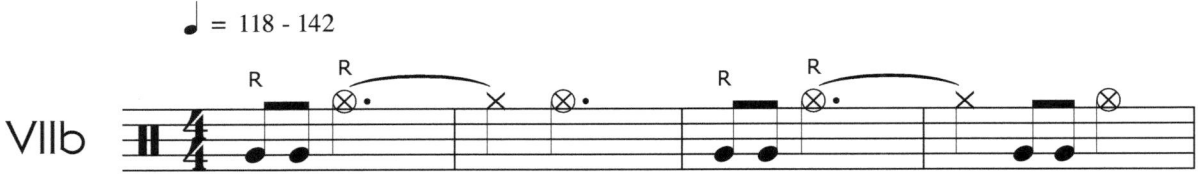

VIIb

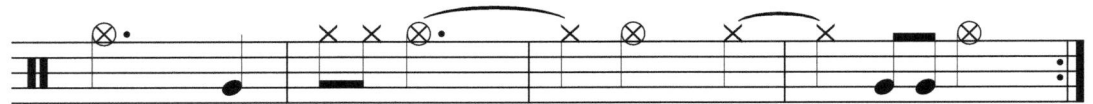

www.ingramcontent.com/pod-product-compliance
Lightning Source LLC
LaVergne TN
LVHW070447070526
838199LV00037B/711